Also by Jim Rogers

A Bull in China
Hot Commodities
Adventure Capitalist
Investment Biker

A GIFT TO MY CHILDREN

A Gift to My Children

A Father's Lessons for
Life and Investing

JIM ROGERS

RANDOM HOUSE

NEW YORK

A Gift to My Children is a commonsense guide to personal finance. In practical advice books, as in life, there are no guarantees, and readers are cautioned to rely on their own judgment about their individual circumstances and to act accordingly.

Published in the United States by Random House, an imprint of The Random House Publishing Group, a division of Random House, Inc., New York.

RANDOM HOUSE and colophon are registered trademarks of Random House, Inc.

LIBRARY OF CONGRESS CATALOGING-IN-PUBLICATION DATA

Rogers, Jim
A gift to my children:
a father's lessons for life and investing / Jim Rogers.
p.   cm.
ISBN 978-1-4000-6754-1
1. Investments. 2 Success. 3 Conduct of life.
4 Success in business. I. Title.
HG4521.R685 2009   650.1—dc22   2008025207

Printed in the United States of America on acid-free paper

www.atrandom.com

8 9 7

Book design by Dana Leigh Blanchette

I owe it all to Paige.
I hope our children have the best of
both worlds: their mother's looks
and their mother's brains.

Preface

Readers of my earlier books will notice right away that this is something different. It concerns neither my adventures traveling the world nor my specific thoughts about the best places to invest your money. Instead it's about the larger lessons that I have distilled from my life experiences—lessons that I think everyone, young and old, will in some ways find more useful than anything I have written before. And that has something to do with the event that spurred me to write it: the birth of my first daughter, Happy, in 2003, and her sister, Baby Bee, who followed in 2008.

I must admit that not very long ago I would have scoffed at even the idea of having children of my own. Growing up in Alabama, I was the oldest of five boys, and as much as I loved my brothers, I spent an awful lot of time looking after them! Also, I couldn't help but notice what a financial burden having five children had imposed on my parents no matter how keen they were on us. Later in life, I was too busy working and traveling even to think about parenthood, which seemed like an endless drain on the time, energy, and money with which I was pursuing my passions. Frankly, sometimes I even felt sorry for people who had kids. How did they have time or money for anything else? *I* was never going to do something so foolish. Boy, was I wrong!

With parenthood, as with investing (and most other things in life), timing is everything. If I'd become a father when I was twenty, thirty, forty—even fifty—it would have been a disaster for me, the mother, and especially for my kids. But now I have the experience, time, and energy to bring to bear on my new passion.

When I was a boy, my father often pulled me aside to convey lessons intended to build what we generally refer to as "character." Often his advice was very simple—work hard, think for yourself, do right by others—but I believe those lessons provided the foundation for everything that has followed in my life. Now that I'm a dad myself, I wanted to put them down in one place, with examples of my own experiences, as a guide to life, adventure, and investing, both for my young daughters and for anyone seeking success in his or her chosen field. I hope that parents will be inspired to give this book to their children, and vice versa, as many of the lessons that I have learned apply not just to young people but to all adults—for example, question everything, never follow the crowd, and beware of boys!

Contents

Introduction

My Dear Daughters,

Your father is an investor, a man who worked hard to learn all that he could to earn enough money to retire early, and, as a result, was able to do so at the age of thirty-seven. I want to share with you what I've learned from all my experiences.

Growing up in the small rural town of Demopolis, all I ever wanted was enough money to ensure my freedom to do what I wanted in life. I had my first job at the age of five, collecting empty soda bottles at the local baseball field. I worked a bunch of other jobs throughout my childhood and eventually made it to Wall Street, where I saw the opportunity to be paid to pursue my passion for traveling all over and understanding the world. And indeed I was: In less than fifteen years, I accumulated enough wealth to retire. Freed from the need to toil in an office, I could go wherever I wished and combine my passions for adventure and for learning all about how the world really worked.

I've always enjoyed working and being successful, but now, what brings me more joy than anything else is my family. I want to share with you those things that are important for you to know so that you too can have happy and successful lives.

A GIFT TO MY CHILDREN

CHAPTER 1

Swim Your Own Races: Do Not Let Others Do Your Thinking for You

RELY ON YOUR OWN INTELLIGENCE.

There are going to be moments in life when you must make very important decisions. You will find many people ready to offer you advice if you ask for it (and even if you don't), but always remember that the life you lead is yours and nobody else's. It's important to decide for yourself what's important to you and what you want before you turn to others. Because while there will be times when outside advice proves wise, there will be at least as many times when it proves utterly useless. The only way to really evaluate other folks' advice is to first learn everything that you can about whatever challenge you are facing. Once you've done that, in most cases you should be able to make an informed decision on your own anyway.

You were born with the ability to decide what is and what isn't in your best interest. Most of the time, you will make the right decision and take the appropriate actions, and in thinking for yourself, you will become far more successful than had you gone against your own judgment. Believe me, I know.

Early on in my investment career, I made the mistake of basing a few important business decisions on colleagues' opinions instead of conducting the research necessary to make an informed decision. It wasn't due to laziness on my part; no one could ever accuse me of that. But, being new to Wall Street, I tended to assume that my more senior colleagues knew more than I did, and so I attributed too much significance to their opinions. You know what happened? Each of those investments ended in failure. Eventually I stopped allowing myself to be influenced by others and began doing the work myself and making my own decisions. Talk about an epiphany. It took me until I was almost thirty years old to realize this—and also to see that it's never too late for a person to change his approach both to business and to life.

I remember once reading a magazine interview with American swimmer Donna de Varona, winner of two gold medals at the 1964 Summer Olympics in Tokyo. The reporter pointed out that earlier in her career, she had been a good swimmer, but not a great one. Now the seventeen-year-old had just placed first in two four-hundred-meter events.

What happened? She replied, "I always used to watch the other swimmers, but then I learned to ignore them and swim my own races."

IF ANYBODY LAUGHS AT YOUR IDEA, VIEW IT AS A SIGN OF POTENTIAL SUCCESS!

If people around you try to discourage you from taking a certain course of action, or ridicule your ideas, take that as a positive sign. Sure it can be difficult not to run with the herd, but the truth is that most long-term success stories are written by folks who've done exactly that. Let me give you an example.

When I was thirty-two years old or so, a Wall Street colleague of mine invited me to join a smart and successful group of financial guys who regularly got together to swap ideas over dinner. At the time, I and a partner were in the early years of our hedge fund called the Quantum Fund. It was a big deal to be invited to these dinners, and, I must admit, I was a little nervous. After all, these were the big guys in my field, and most of them had a great deal more experience than I did.

We were sitting in the private room of a fancy midtown Manhattan restaurant when the host asked each guest at the table to recommend an investment. Most of them touted so-called growth stocks. When my turn came, I recommended Lockheed, the aerospace company. Once extremely prosperous, by the 1970s it had fallen on hard times. A fellow sitting opposite me smirked and, making sure that I heard him, stage-whispered, "Who buys stocks like this? Why buy a bankrupt company?"

About six years later, I ran into this schoolyard bully. I resisted the urge to remind him of his condescending remark. It wasn't easy, given that the stock had risen many, many times in value, and for all the reasons that I had explained over dinner: The company shed a huge money-losing division and instead concentrated on the exciting new area of electronic warfare systems. Furthermore, as could have been predicted, defense spending had grown rapidly following a period of decline.

I had a similar experience with my investments in China. People used to call the country a graveyard for investors, and as recently as the late 1990s, few Westerners invested there. But those who did made a fortune. What did I know that others didn't? Well, back in the 1980s, I sensed China's potential and decided to learn everything I could about it and start investing my money there. Many people told me I was insane; that the rigidly Communist Chinese government would confiscate money earned by successful people, especially outsiders. But I followed my instincts, learned as much as I could about political trends in China, and studied as many documents as I could find. Most valuable of all, I drove across the country—and it's a *big* country—several times. Here's what I learned by seeing it with my own eyes:

China had more than one billion workers, and over one-third of their annual income went into savings. That's astoundingly high. In contrast, the savings rate in the United States was a mere 4 percent. (Today it's just half that, at 2 percent.) Everywhere I traveled, I saw that the capitalism, drive, and entrepreneurship that had characterized China for centuries had at long last reemerged following the failure of Communism. And there was no going back.

I was struck by how the Chinese people worked from dawn to dusk. In one town, I met a farmer known locally as the "Apple King" because of his huge orchards. In another town, I talked to a successful restaurateur-hotelier who proudly told me how he'd started out by selling bread to farmers as they walked to work every day at dawn. China's cities were full of college kids determined to forge their own futures and enjoy greater prosperity than their parents' generation. People were learning English and Japanese instead of Russian; they could see who had the money. Meanwhile, the Western media persisted in referring to the country as "Mao Tse-tung's China," even though the Communist dictator had died in 1976. They were blind to the changes taking place—and I would have been too, had I not gone there myself and immersed myself in Chinese society. I came away thinking, *How could a country like this* not *grow?* Since then, China's economic development has far exceeded not only that of the United States but of nearly every other nation in the world.

BE WHO YOU ARE. BE ORIGINAL! BE BOLD!

Take a good look at men and women who have been successful in their fields. Now, anyone can get lucky once, but I'm talking about people with a sustained record of success. Whether they are artists or musicians, high school teachers or college professors, they all approach their work in a refreshingly original way. This is true of companies too. For example, look at Apple Computer. Steve Jobs and Company refused to accept the conventional wisdom that they would be flattened by the giants IBM and Microsoft. Apple continued to produce high-quality, innovative products and has since been removed from the corporate endangered-species list. In fact, the company is thriving.

I want you to pursue your own desires and aspirations with that kind of courage and devotion. Your father succeeded as an investor, but that doesn't mean that you must be investors too. What I want is for both of you to be your true, original, unique selves. No one ever became a standout success by imitating others.

ABOVE ALL, BE ETHICAL.

As you continue to grow to adulthood, I will continue to offer you guidance. There may be times when I disagree with your choices, but you do not have to accept my advice merely because I am your father. I look at you as independent human beings. Others may say that you are too young to decide for yourselves. I say do what you want, as long as you use your own judgment to determine what is right ethically.

But while you need not concern yourself with conventional wisdom and other so-called established notions, you must respect and follow the rules, laws, and ethical practices without which society cannot exist. This is expected of everyone. It is not simply the proper way to live, it's the smart way. Honorable people don't find themselves entangled in legal problems, and they always come out on top in the long run. There are smart people who have gotten themselves in serious trouble because they tried to make money the easy way, or sometimes illegally. Had they applied themselves, they probably would have earned even greater profits legally.

SAVE.

You will meet people who will urge you to spend your money freely; they will tell you, "You can't take it with you!" As you get older, you will probably have friends who eat at expensive restaurants every night, buy the latest gadgets or fashion trends, and spend vacations at fancy beach resorts. You must avoid the trap of spending money willy-nilly simply because you can. Not only is this a road to financial ruin, it can cause you to forget what's important in life.

I am not saying that you should never travel or buy anything nice. I am merely suggesting that you should think

wisely about whether the thing you are contemplating doing
or buying is really worthwhile or whether its benefits will be,
at best, fleeting. I was once married to a woman who was always nagging me to buy a new sofa, a new TV, and so on. I'd
explain that if we saved and invested wisely, one day we
could afford ten sofas or whatever. Needless to say, we did
not stay married long, and now I am lucky to have your
mother, who shares the same attitude toward personal fi-
nances.

Happy, you already have five piggy banks, and you love
putting money into them. Please continue to save. Those
who save and invest wisely will face fewer financial woes
throughout life. And please help us teach your new sister,
Baby Bee, the importance of saving.

CHAPTER 2

Focus on What You Like

AGE IS IRRELEVANT WHEN YOU ARE
PASSIONATE ABOUT A GOAL.

I started my first business in 1948 at the age of six. Perhaps a little young to be an entrepreneur, you might think, but age is irrelevant when you're passionate about something. Instead of playing baseball with my friends, I much preferred spending my time collecting empty bottles at their games, to pick up a little cash. When my father offered to loan me money to start my own business, I jumped at it. I bought a peanut parcher for $100—a huge sum in the backwoods of Alabama—and was highly successful selling peanuts and drinks at Little League games. I hustled throughout the stands, trying to get in as many sales as I could before the games ended, and before too long, I hired my brothers and friends to sell too. After five years, I paid off the loan from my father and still had $100 in my bank account.

In graduate school at Oxford University, I realized that I liked investing better than being an entrepreneur. I'd used my scholarship funds to buy a little stock in IBM and was quickly hooked. When you find something that interests you, do not let your age hold you back. Be bold and, in the words of the Nike sports-apparel company, just do it.

DEDICATE YOURSELF TO WHAT YOU FEEL PASSIONATE ABOUT.

Where should a person start in order to be successful? The answer is easy: Try as many things as you can, then pursue the one (or two, or three) about which you're passionate. I became successful in investing because this is what I enjoyed most. But if you love cooking, open up your own restaurant. Learn to dance if that is your forte. Become a gardener if that is your passion. Maybe someday you might want to open a chain of gardening shops. The quickest way to success is to do what you like and give it your best.

For me, my love for investing was linked to my fascination with researching and learning in detail what was happening in different parts of the world. As a student, even as far back as grammar school, I loved to learn about other countries, including their history. On Wall Street, I realized that people would actually pay money for such knowledge; for example, that the price of copper would rise because a revolution was coming in Chile.

The least-happy people I know are those stuck in jobs they don't love; many because they can't imagine giving up a paycheck. In elementary school, I had a teacher named Mrs. Martin, who brought to life every subject she taught. She always seemed happy and excited to see us. This was in a rural town in a state with the lowest teachers' salaries in the whole country! I've rarely met someone so happy and so dedicated as Mrs. Martin, and she clearly received a great deal of satisfaction from her job.

Even early on, I would have worked for free had I been able to afford it. People who follow their passions do not "go to work." They get up each day and cannot wait to have more fun doing what they love to do. I'm an investor. If I'd tried to do something else, like becoming a doctor, or a fashion designer, or who knows what, my life wouldn't have turned out nearly as well. (*Especially* if I'd chosen fashion design. Even now I never know which colors go together; thank goodness for your mother.) That is why I say it is best to start with something that interests you and that you truly enjoy. Even if you don't become wealthy pursuing your passions, you will be rich in satisfaction. Plus, you'll be happy. You can't put a price on that. You are also more likely to become successful if you do what you love.

CHAPTER 3

Good Habits for Life and Investing

BE A SELF-STARTER.

At fourteen, I spent my Saturday mornings working for my Uncle Chink—who had been called this since the 1920s because Alabama people thought he looked Chinese—preposterous, looking back on it now. He owned a tiny convenience store across the street from a stockyard and a factory. The workers used to amble in to buy sandwiches, cigarettes, chewing tobacco—that kind of store. My job was to help wait on customers and stock the shelves. Sometimes business was slow, but I never sat idle, in part because of some advice from my father, Jim Sr., the manager of the Borden Chemical plant in town.

"There is always something you can be doing," he used to say. "When there's nothing else to do, dust the shelves." And that's exactly what I did. My initiative so impressed my uncle that he gave me a raise without my having to ask for one. That came as a big surprise, since Uncle Chink was not exactly known to be loose with money.

Three or four years later, I brought the same energy to a job I obtained with Mr. Brooker, a local home builder. At first, I couldn't even hammer a nail straight, and the men on the job weren't shy about pointing this out. But when we were awaiting deliveries of building materials or had nothing to do, I'd gather up the scrap lumber or sweep up the sawdust or whatever else I could find. "Say what you want," the contractor told them, "but this kid never stops. He has the right attitude, he has the proper approach, and I want him working for me." Eventually I did learn to drive nails as quickly as anyone, dig foundations, install roofs, and all the other skills necessary to do the job. If it weren't for my work ethic, I might never have gotten the chance.

ATTENTION TO DETAILS IS WHAT SEPARATES
SUCCESS FROM FAILURE.

If you love and care about what you do, you will naturally want to do it the best that you can. In investing, as in life, the small details often spell the difference between success and failure. So you must be attentive! However trivial it may seem, you must research and check each and every piece of information you need to make a decision. Leave no questions or nagging feelings of uncertainty uninvestigated. The most common reason why people do not succeed is that their research is faulty or limited to the confines of what is immediately available. Only through meticulous research will you obtain the knowledge necessary for success. It requires abundant work and diligence, but the effort will give you a distinct advantage over your competitors.

When I was an undergrad at Yale University, a fellow history major asked me how many hours I'd studied for a recent exam. "I put in five hours," he said, very satisfied with himself. I couldn't give him an exact number, since I'd never *stopped* studying. Arriving at Yale from rural Alabama, I was in over my head, to tell you the truth. Most of the other students had attended elite prep schools and were far better prepared than I was. My advantage, though, turned out to be that I worked much harder than they did. For me, there was no such thing as "enough." No finish line.

If and when you decide to pursue investing or whatever your fancy, do not underestimate the value of due diligence. Look through each and every financial statement you can get your hands on, including the detailed notes. If you just read the annual reports of companies, you will have done more than 98 percent of investors. If you read the notes of the financial statements, you will be ahead of 99.5 percent. Verify those financial statements, as well as future projections announced by the top executives, by doing your own legwork. Talk to customers, suppliers, competitors, and anyone else who might affect the company. Do not invest unless you can say with absolute certainty that you are more knowledgeable about this particular firm than 98 percent of Wall Street analysts. Believe me, it can be done. But only with the extra effort.

In the 1960s, General Motors was the world's most successful company, and everyone coveted its stock. One day a GM analyst went to the board of directors with the message "The Japanese are coming." They ignored him. In fact, they didn't even bother to listen to him. Investors who did broad homework sold their high-value General Motors stock then and there and bought Toyota instead. The Japanese were building smaller, more efficient, and extremely reliable cars, which quickly found a huge market worldwide, including here in the States. U.S. car manufacturers had been dictating to the marketplace rather than listening to their customers. They've been forced to play catch-up to their Japanese counterparts ever since.

Here's another example: As recently as the 1990s, there was no better value on Wall Street than Sears. Its stock always seemed cheap, but few were even aware of a growing discount company called Wal-Mart; they never bothered to examine what was happening in small towns throughout the United States. Those who did began to buy stock in Wal-Mart instead of in Sears, JCPenney, and all the other good-value stores.

When investing widely in a particular nation, begin by checking the strength of the country's basic institutions.

Does it have respect for the rule of law? Does it crack down on corruption? Does the legal system facilitate ethical corporate behavior? You cannot do this by simply reading articles in magazines and newspapers. You must go to the country yourself and see, for example, if there is a currency black market. If one exists, then you know that the country has problems. Black market exchange rates exist only when the government is imposing artificial controls. The difference in parity between the official currency rate and the black market rate indicates the gravity of the problem in that nation. It is symptomatic. The higher the fever, the worse the sickness; in other words, the greater the gap in parity, the deeper the problem.

During my first motorcycle circumnavigation in 1990 and 1991, I looked forward to spending time in Algeria, my second stop in Africa. I had every intention of investing there. But once I discovered that the country had a currency black market with a 100 percent premium—well, I lost interest real quickly. Algeria's problems came to the fore in the next few years. I later figured out there were absurd price controls and a government printing huge amounts of money to pay its bills. Workers, merchants, and everyone else were being squeezed. It was no surprise that voters soon elected a protest party that was then overthrown by a military coup. Investing in countries or anything else when easily observable information suggests doing the opposite can be a brilliant strategy, but only if your own deeper analysis shows positive change around the corner. Be careful! At the turn of the millennium, the African nation of Zimbabwe was a major agricultural exporter that also sold coal and other minerals abroad. Its currency was stable, and the stock market attracted investors to some sound companies. Since then, however, the political situation in Zimbabwe has deteriorated badly, pulling down the economy. Now the country, riddled with violence and corruption, is desperately begging for food handouts, exports have plummeted almost to zero, and the annual rate of inflation is over *200,000 percent.* The government just prints money to reward its friends, so that money there loses its value literally overnight.

LIVE YOUR LIFE WITH A DREAM.

In addition to finding a fulfilling vocation, you must have a dream. In my younger years, I thought that making money was fun, but I didn't really have a plan beyond that. Had I continued down that path, I would have lost interest by now. Investing around the world exposed me to a range of cultures and different people. Eventually I realized that my dream was to seek adventure and learn about the world by seeing as much of it as I could. So, at the age of thirty-seven, I began traveling the globe on a motorcycle.

You see, when you begin something, you may not always have a concrete picture or vision of the future. But if you continue to be passionate and work hard at what you truly love to do, then you will eventually find that dream. Which may morph into yet *another* dream. And another. At this point in my life, you, my daughters, are my focus and passion. That is why I spend every moment possible with you. You are my dream today, and all I want is for both of you to do what you love and live smart, interesting lives with a dream.

CHAPTER 4

Common Sense? Not So Common

MOST PERCEIVED WISDOM IS
A MISCONCEPTION.

I've written about the need to follow your own intelligence, to think for yourself. As you travel the journey called life, you will come across conventional wisdom—accepted "truths" about how to behave, or what to study, or eat, or how to invest. You must remember never blindly to accept what you hear or read, no matter how many people believe it or how strongly they advocate it. Always consider alternative interpretations. The popular beliefs embraced by the larger society are often mistaken. I want to explain how to make sense of "common sense."

Here's a good example of conventional wisdom being wildly inaccurate: In the early 1970s, stock prices in the defense industry plummeted because of cuts in U.S. defense spending. Some contractors verged on bankruptcy (among them, Lockheed). No one dared invest in defense, especially with conventional wisdom decreeing that defense shares would continue to fall.

But if you analyzed the reasons for the defense industry's recent free fall, you didn't have to be a sage to foresee a brighter future. For one thing, the absurd protracted war in Vietnam, which finally ended in 1973, had decimated U.S. military strength. That it would need a drastic overhaul, and soon, was driven home ominously later the same year with the Arab-Israeli War. That conflict on the other side of the globe opened America's government's eyes to how inadequately prepared we were to protect ourselves and our allies. Our government began pouring money into defense once again, jump-starting those companies' stocks. Some increased in value by as much as a hundredfold in the next decade or so—the exact opposite of what so many analysts had fiercely predicted.

Another example: In 1970 crude oil sold for under $3 a barrel. Most experts believed that the price would remain low for the foreseeable future. Many were convinced that new technologies, with impressive-sounding names such as diamond drill bits, deep drilling, and offshore platforms, combined with major oil discoveries in Alaska, Mexico, and the North Sea, all but ensured low prices. Careful research, however, showed that our supply of oil could not possibly meet the world's increasing demand. Basic Economics 101 told you that crude oil prices were destined to rise considerably.

Accordingly, I invested in oil around 1971. Ten years later, oil was up to $35 a barrel. By then, of course, everyone was investing in oil (including the same folks who had underrated its value). Clearly, the market had overheated. We had a boom in exploration, and those new oil fields discovered in the sixties began coming to market. At the same time, demand slowed, as many people started to become more energy conscious, buying fuel-efficient cars and adjusting their thermostats at home. In 1978 oil production actually exceeded consumption for the first time in years. I sold my shares and did not buy oil again until 1998. Anyone who has been to a pump lately knows what has happened since then.

THE MEDIA OFTEN PROPAGATES CONVENTIONAL WISDOM.

You should read the newspaper every day, but approach it—and all media, for that matter—with a healthy sense of skepticism. When I was young, newspapers were revered as impartial sources of news and, more so than today, many of them were. But like all purveyors of conventional wisdom, they sometimes fall into the trap of reporting information peddled by self-interested people or failing to dig deep

enough for the facts. More than once, I'd find myself making investment judgments based on suspect information or
weak reporting.

I have since learned how better to judge the content
of stories in the media, occasionally turning their inaccura-
cies to my advantage. In cases where I'm making an investment decision (or a decision about for whom to vote,
et cetera), I cross-check information from the media with
other available sources including government reports, international organizations, company reports, competitive
views—whatever I can find. I scan the copy closely for language that sounds like it came straight off a company press
release. And I carefully analyze any statistical arguments to
see whether the claim being made is based on sound statistical logic.

When I was a guest professor of finance at Columbia
University in the 1980s, my students often seemed surprised
by how much detail I brought to bear on making decisions,
but this is the basic tool of anyone hoping to transcend conventional wisdom. I will read any document I can get my
hands on. If I have doubts about things I see on TV or read
in the paper, then I go wherever I need to go in the world to
investigate. Seeking out multiple perspectives on the same
story will always help you figure out the truth.

Of course, here in the twenty-first century, we are del-
uged with information, much of it from dubious (and bi-
ased) sources. It's surprising to me that so few people seem
to bother to confirm the information they're about to use to

reach key decisions. It was the French writer Voltaire, in his *Dictionnaire Philosophique,* who said: "Common sense is not so common." And as U.S. Army general George Patton once put it, "If everyone is thinking the same thing, someone is not thinking."

CHAPTER 5

Your Education, Part I: Let the World Be a Part of Your Perspective

DO NOT RELY ON BOOKS; GO AND SEE THE WORLD!

Travel and see the world extensively. You will broaden your perspective many times over. If you really want to know yourself and your country, go see the world.

Your father can say this with conviction because I have been around the world twice. Beginning in 1990, I spent twenty-two months traveling through six continents on a motorcycle. On my second trip, which started in 1999, your mother and I traveled a total of 245,000 kilometers in a special Mercedes through 116 different countries for three years. We saw with our own eyes diverse lands and nationalities. In the course of our travels, we were offered any number of delicacies, including a live snake for dinner. It was slaughtered and prepared before our eyes. And I loved it!

We drove through war zones in Angola, Western Sahara, India, Sudan, and other parts of the world. In fact, we made it a point to visit the "frightening" parts of cities to see if they were really dangerous. You know what we learned? That people everywhere are basically the same, no matter their ethnic group, language, religion, food, or dress. We learned that there is no reason to fear foreigners or foreign peoples.

You will discover more about yourself as you encounter and experience the world's diversity. You will develop interests that you never entertained before and recognize your strengths and weaknesses. You will realize that some things that you'd thought were important are of little consequence. What you wear or who you know or where you dine or from where you originate may mean less. I was once a baseball fanatic but now know nothing about the game.

It's important that you not simply visit other countries as a tourist. Yes, do see the monuments and eat at predicable restaurants, but also see for yourself how different people live. Experience life as they do; see the world from the ground up. By observing ordinary life rather than merely visiting tourist attractions, you will forever be stumbling upon experiences that will raise important questions in your mind.

The English author and poet Rudyard Kipling wrote in his poem "The English Flag," "What can he know of England who only England knows?" I urge you to leave your country for a few years. You can always return, but you will have a new understanding. Of everything. The knowledge and experiences you will have gained will benefit you in untold ways, making you a better person, worker, and even parent. Our family is American, and we will continue to spend a good deal of time there, but we have moved to Asia to help give you as much exposure as possible to the bigger world beyond U.S. borders.

UNDERSTAND THE SIGNIFICANCE OF BRICS.

While a student at the University of Oxford in the 1960s, I managed my own scholarship money until the deadline for paying tuition rolled around. By that time, I had already developed a basic approach to investing; an important part of that was developing a global perspective.

Nowadays you can hardly pick up a business publication without seeing a reference to "BRICs," a popular acronym in the world of investing. BRICs refers to a thesis currently popular with investors and politicians that Brazil, Russia, India, and China are destined to be the world's leading economies by the year 2050, and therefore are rife with investment opportunities. I'll tell you a bit more about what I think about each of these countries, but the larger point is the importance of focusing investment strategies on growing economies abroad.

As anyone who has met me knows, my experience and time spent traveling leads me to feel bullish about Brazil and China, bearish about Russia, and skeptical about India.

The situation in Brazil will improve significantly over the next fifteen years, as the country increases production of commodities such as sugar and iron ore. Sugar, a major export, happens to be the raw material not just of candy but also of ethanol, which right now is considered to be an attractive alternative energy source to crude oil. Although I'm bullish about these commodity markets, I am neutral about Brazil's stock market at the moment and its currency, the real.

Next up for discussion: Russia. Why my skepticism of that country? Despite its abundant natural resources, the fundamentals, or basic economic conditions, simply aren't there. The capitalism that now exists in Russia is *outlaw* capitalism. What's more, the USSR has broken up into fifteen countries already and will continue to splinter into as many as fifty or one hundred countries in the not-too-distant future. There were 124 ethnic, linguistic, and religious groups in the land, and few of them are happy being part of a republic dictated to by the old Union of Soviet Socialist Republics.

In reality, Russia is still an underdeveloped nation, much better than when I first visited in 1966, but still not first world. I was there in 1990, just as the USSR was on the verge of dissolving, and again in 1999, with your mother. We heard bombs exploding while dining in Moscow as Putin's forces were consolidating power. The country is plagued by far more bombings and assassinations than is reported in the Western media. I predict that the current violence will escalate to an eventual catastrophe. President Vladimir Putin (presently incognito as prime minister) may control Moscow and St. Petersburg, but not much else, while the Russian Mafia exerts a stranglehold elsewhere. An investor can profit there, but only if he's in cahoots with the criminal element. If he operates outside the Mob, money troubles may be the least of his worries. Many foreign companies have learned by now that the Russians will take assets away whenever they like, either by taxation or by brute force. Actually, the situation in Russia is one of the reasons why I am so bullish about commodities: There is simply no way that we can expect an increased supply of raw materials from there anytime soon.

More bad news from the Russian front: Parts of Russia itself are straining to gain independence, as are parts of other former Soviet republics. The Ukraine, for example, could split at any time. Some will disagree with me, but I always point to the example of Chechnya, a small republic, about the size of Connecticut, in southern Russia. The Red Army has been trying to control Chechnya's population of only one and a half million for about fifteen years, with little success. What more do you need to know? There is no Red Army anymore—certainly not one that can hold together the country's vast expanses.

But wait? Isn't capitalism making inroads in Russia, just like in China? Sorry, but there's a huge difference between the two. Unlike China, Russia doesn't utilize its capital efficiently. Productivity levels are low, since the country tries to compete using the same infrastructure and factories built under Communist rule, with few upgrades and little modification. Furthermore, whereas Chinese citizens who study or live overseas bring back capital and know-how, Russians who leave rarely return to contribute to the country's rehabilitation.

As for India, I have observed firsthand its stifling bureaucracy, and its lack of infrastructure, especially when compared to China. The country's national highway is a two-lane road that was built decades ago and is now full of potholes, not to mention traffic, wagons, animals, pedestrians, drying vegetables, carts, breakdowns, and everything else under the sun. I had to purchase multiple cell phones there while on our trip, because each was usable only in certain areas of India. The only business to be privatized between 1991 and 2001 was a bakery. The situation is slowly improving, but it is often one step backward for every step forward. As a result, I simply am not motivated to buy into India. But as I've stressed, don't just take it from me! Keep an eye on India. If I am wrong, and it really does change, it could be a great opportunity—for investors and, most of all, for the people of India.

BE OPEN TO PEOPLE WHO ARE DIFFERENT, WHETHER AT HOME OR ABROAD.

Demopolis, the name of the town where I grew up, means "city of the people." But back then, people of color weren't included. Like most other places in Alabama and across the South, Demopolis was segregated. There was the white part of town, and the black part. Which also happened to be the poor section.

I have to admit, in my early years, I didn't think about the injustice of this too much. It was just how things were. We didn't know anything different. In fact, my family hardly knew any black people at all, and I had not a single black friend. But once I became a teenager, in the mid-1950s, I started to see things differently. My Uncle Chink's general store happened to be in the black part of Demopolis. One day I was handing out advertising leaflets when I observed something I'd never seen before: A Japanese woman was living in the black section solely because she had married an African-American GI. Had she married a white U.S. soldier, of course, she could have lived anywhere she wanted. She would have been exactly the same person yet would have had an entirely different life. That's when I started to realize that there had to be something seriously wrong with a system that kept people apart based on the color of their skin.

Fifty years later, I'm seeing a disturbing trend in America. Fear of terrorism and anger over the struggling economy have fueled what I sense to be a growing sentiment of isolationism and xenophobia among some of our leaders and citizens. We should close off the United States, they say, to foreign ideas, capital, products, and—predictably—people. Other countries are starting to follow suit. Now, the world has prospered mightily since the end of World War II, when we in the West vowed not to close ourselves off from the rest of the world, as happened in the 1930s with disastrous results. While Nazi Germany systematically invaded Czechoslovakia, then Poland, then France, then Russia, as part of its grand plan to conquer Europe, a war-weary America resisted its European allies' pleas to join their fight. By the time the United States did finally enter the war two years after it had begun, and only after Japan's surprise attack on Pearl Harbor, her military at first was no match for the German and Japanese war machines, which had spent the previous decade ratcheting up for battle. Unfortunately, too few of us today understand the lessons of history; the results will not be pretty if we repeat the isolationist policies of the 1930s.

After World War II, the world vowed never again to allow the protectionism and "beggar thy neighbor" policies that had led to the Depression and world war. The General Agreement on Tariffs and Trade (GATT) was signed, opening trade and financial flows. The world has had several decades of unprecedented growth and expansion as a result. The WTO has succeeded GATT in attempting to continue the spread of trade and prosperity.

The people who designed GATT are all dead and few now read or understand history. Protectionism and isolationism are rising again. Many nations are saying, "If the United States can do it, so can we." Difficult economic times often give birth to dangerous policies, and may again. Remember that history "rhymes" and be attentive; economic problems and war have recurred throughout history, so prepare yourself in case these tendencies persist. You may have to move to neutral countries while making investments that could benefit from turmoil, such as real assets and freely convertible currencies.

KEEP AN OPEN MIND AND
BE A WORLD CITIZEN!

You were born into a generation that pollster John Zogby has called "the first global citizens." Your peer group is more open-minded and more globally minded than any generation that preceded it. This is remarkable, and it will greatly expand your possibilities for personal and professional happiness.

Keeping an open mind includes never closing yourself to the possibility that people are different from what you first imagined. It is natural, and often useful, to form ideas about people based on the limited information we have when we meet, from what we observe, and the details they provide. But there's a world of difference between knowing a *type* and knowing a *person*. When you've traveled all over the planet, as I have, and communicate with people from other cultures, you come to understand that, ultimately, very few human beings conform to the stereotypes imposed upon them. And, for the most part, we all want the same things out of life.

In 1960, when I decided to leave Demopolis for Yale University—in the North!—many of my neighbors could not understand why I would want to do such a thing. Most of them had never been outside of Alabama, much less the South. But I'll tell you, in addition to all of the fascinating people I met in New Haven, Connecticut, and later in New York City, some of the most interesting people to me were ones I had not known before from my hometown. Everyone I met knew who I was, but I didn't know them, because of segregation.

Understand this: If everyone saw himself as a citizen of the world rather than of his town, city, or country, the world would be a more peaceful, better place where success in all forms is abundant and available to all. That's not to say that we can't be patriotic and love our country. But we must always be open to those who are different, because people from different backgrounds have much to teach us, and vice versa.

When your mother and I were traveling the world, we constantly met people who were afraid of those who were different—be it religion, language, ethnicity, or skin color—until they interacted with them, and laughed and swapped stories. Wars are not started by groups of people who know one another and suddenly decide to destroy one another. Twenty-year-olds prefer playing, dancing, dining, drinking, or debating with one another and will do so if given the opportunity. This has been true throughout history. It is flawed politicians who inevitably fail the kids, appeal to their worst instincts, and have them killing one another needlessly.

I was instantly shocked when I first saw the wall of the Chapel at Balliol College Oxford on my arrival. There were lists of all the graduates who had died in World War I. There were a few dozen young British soldiers, but my shock was when I realized there were also a dozen or so young Germans. They had been university students together until some bungling politicians absurdly sent them off to kill one another in the mud instead of playing football together, which would have made more sense for the world—and for them.

As you get older and read history, you will learn that war has never been good for any nation, even the ones that "win." If you are ever in a country that descends into war, I suggest you leave until it is over. Truth is always the first casualty of war, so you need to get your distance.

A Nobel Prize–winning poet used this epitaph for his son, who had been killed in the senseless First World War:

> *If any question why we died*
> *Tell them, because our fathers lied.*

Your father and all of our forebears in America, for a few centuries now, have served in the military, but you should not. Break the chain and live away from wars.

My wish, as your father, is that you become a world citizen by your own will and decision. Someday I hope to see you take that first bold step.

Of all the adventures I have had in my life, you, my daughters, are the ultimate adventure. You already show me a new world. If fatherhood enriches one's travels, I am certain that the reverse is also true. I think of all the things that I have gained from my travels that I will now be able to give to you. I cannot wait to show you how to drive, how to read a map—things my father taught me. After English, what languages will you learn? From birth, a Chinese governess has taught you Mandarin and Tang dynasty poems and Chinese characters. I hope to add Spanish to the mix soon.

I think of all the places that I *haven't* been: the interior of Brazil, southern India, Eritrea, Iran, Israel. These and other places I will show you. Your mother and I explored moving to Shanghai or Spain, and spending time in Punta del Este, Uruguay, or Cochabamba, Bolivia. Because I am so optimistic about Asia, we chose to educate you in Singapore for many reasons including a bilingual culture, great education, the world's best health care, efficiency, et cetera, everything works. Japan has been the most successful country of the past fifty years, China of the past thirty years, and Singapore of the past forty years. We hope you will always view the whole world as your home and not be so hidebound that you limit your horizons and possibilities. Be eager to move if you see opportunities. Just as our forebears did. We hope that you will learn here in Singapore, but who knows? We are also exploring a home in Vienna, Austria, since we love it so much. Perhaps you will grow up in one of those other places. Or maybe I will buy a rocking chair and sing "Ol' Man River," rearing a family where my father reared his in America's rural South. I suspect my father would have liked that—and, in his wisdom, might have wanted it all along.

Your grandfather died at the age of eighty-three in 2001, before you were born. It is one of my regrets that you will never meet him. You can see in his photos that he was of average height and build, but you cannot see his intensity. He was a stern disciplinarian, and I wish I were as disciplined with you. He made sure that my brothers and I knew that we had to do what needed to be done. Slacking off or putting things off until later? Unheard of in our house. As the manager of a chemical plant, he spent many, many hours at work. All five of his sons are hard workers.

Dad also made sure that we knew to save as much money as possible because nothing would ever be given to us. His father had died young in a coal mine he owned in 1929, then his mother lost it all in the Great Depression of the 1930s. He was a real son of the Depression and reared us accordingly. I now understand how focused he was on his five sons and how much he sacrificed for us. I'm like him in many respects. For instance, I rarely bother to buy new clothes. I just like old clothes better, but now I wonder if I inherited that trait from him, because he was always trying to give us more.

Your mother and I always worry that we might give you too much or make things too easy for you, since we do not want to spoil you. If my father were still alive, he wouldn't have spoiled you at all, but he would have tried to do whatever he could for you.

CHAPTER 6

Your Education, Part II:
Learn Philosophy; Learn to "Think"

PHILOSOPHY WILL TEACH YOU HOW TO
THINK FOR YOURSELF.

Happy, you were born in May 2003; Baby Bee, in March 2008. Although it's a little too early now, I hope that you will study philosophy someday. You must learn to think at a profound level if you want to understand yourself and what's important to you. You must know yourself if you want to accomplish anything in life. Studying philosophy has helped me do just this.

I am not talking about the complex logic that is characteristic of philosophy and that intimidates many people; I am referring to the simple art of thinking for yourself. So many folks today are caught up in conventional thinking, their intellectual processes circumscribed by such concepts as the state, culture, or religion. To think outside the established framework, to examine things independently—this is true philosophy. Studying philosophy trains a person to examine every concept and every "fact."

Studying philosophy at Oxford University was a struggle for me, because they were always asking me abstract questions—such basic things as whether the sun will always rise in the east or does a tree crashing in an isolated forest make a sound. Frankly, back then I just did not see the purpose of a lot of it, but I've since come to understand the need to examine everything, no matter how accepted or proven. The ability to seek other explanations and to think around corners will serve you well.

DO CURRENT WRITINGS ON PHILOSOPHY HELP US LEARN TO THINK?

To engage in philosophical thinking and to read books on philosophy are not the same things. True, reading helps develop our ability to think, but more effort is required to really sharpen the faculty.

Here's an exercise: Reflect on situations where conventional wisdom and custom turned out to be wrong. Take the time to find out what actually happened. This will help you to develop knowledge and confidence, so that the next time a decision is required, you will be able to constructively analyze the assumption of the majority.

THE TWO WAYS OF THINKING.

There are two methods of examination that are particularly useful in all walks of life, including investing. One is to draw conclusions from your observations, and the other is to proceed solely on the basis of logic.

Drawing a conclusion from observations is very simple. When you examine the history of the stock market, for instance, you see that the bull alternates between stocks and commodities. Historically, this has happened in cycles of fifteen to twenty-three years. The commodities market became bullish in 1999, so I expect this trend to continue. Based on historical precedent, the commodity bull may run until sometime between 2014 and 2022, although there will be some serious setbacks along the way. For example, in 1987 stock markets around the world collapsed 40 percent to 80 percent, scaring everyone to death, but it was far from the end of the multiyear bull market. In the 1970s gold at one point went up 600 percent before beginning to react. It consolidated and declined 50 percent over a two-year period, causing many to give up. It then turned around and rose 850 percent. That is how markets work: They make most of us look foolish much of the time.

Now I will give you an illustration of what it means to

infer by logic alone. I can't prove it, but I have come up with
my own theory about the interplay between stocks and commodities. Take a look at Kellogg's, which boasts the world's
largest share in cereal. Cereals are made from commodities
such as rice, wheat, corn, and sugar. When there is a downturn in the commodities market, the cost of these foods
drops. Provided that sales levels are sustained, the company's net profit goes up, which in turn is reflected in a rise
in its share price. However, when the price of commodities
rises, Kellogg's cannot reflect its cost increase in the price of
its cereals immediately. This will affect the company's net
profit, and its stock price will suffer as a consequence. Companies benefit from low costs when commodities are slug-
gish, and when commodity prices rise, profits drop off,
taking stock prices with them. As you can see, it is a good
mental exercise to figure out how commodities and stocks
are inversely correlated.

Two ways of thinking: The former is called induction
(proceeding from a specific conclusion to more general observations), and the latter, deduction (proceeding from general evidence to a specific truth). Neither method is better
than the other. What is important is that you train yourself
to apply both, so that you can think in a balanced way.

DON'T NEGLECT THE BEAR.

What is it that most investors fail to consider? Most look for
the bull and neglect the bear. As an investor, I am always in

search of "what is bearish." When people are crazed about an overheated market and are oblivious of other investment possibilities, *that's* when I find a good deal.

During the stock bubble of 1998, when most people ignored commodities, I started up a commodity index. Commodities had been in the doldrums for years, so no one had made any money. Most people fled the field, and few young people even studied natural resources. Fewer still went into farming or mining (MBAs were all the rage then, remember?), the end result being that we currently have a shortage of farmers and geologists. That is true in other countries as well. These factors led to a multiyear decline in productive capacity, while demand kept rising. The returns show how well commodities have done. The Rogers International Commodity Index, which I founded in 1998, quadrupled over the next ten years, while the Standard and Poor's 500 index of stocks rose about 40 percent.

CHAPTER 7

Your Education, Part III:
Learn History!

A MACROSCOPIC VIEW OF THE WORLD
IS WHAT YOU NEED.

I want you to study history. I want you to understand the changes taking place in the world from a *macroscopic* perspective; by that, I mean that I want you to understand the big picture of how the world works and has always worked. You will learn that what is true today may not be true in twenty years, or even ten. In 1910 the British and German royal families were the fastest of friends and allies. Four years later their countries were embroiled in a totally senseless war. Examine the world at any one point, and you will find that ten to twenty years later much had changed. Think of any year and see how much the world changed in just the next ten years—much less twenty years. Say 1960 or 1970 or 1980 or 1990. Just pick any year you like and see how extraordinarily the world changed. It will happen throughout your lifetimes, too.

An interest in history, politics, and economics will help you see how occurrences in one country affect other nations as well, economically and in other ways. For instance, a single country's political turmoil can drive up commodity prices around the world; the price of gold in particular will usually rise. A full-scale war will drive up not only the price of gold but the price of most other commodities.

WHICH HISTORY BOOK TELLS US THE TRUTH?

History is multifaceted. There are historical studies in economics and politics; there is history as examined and understood from the viewpoint of the United States, from a European perspective, and from the outlook of various Asian, African, and South American nations. You will learn that most history is written by victors so has a clear view. As long as the historian has been rigorous, each perspective can fill in a piece of the historical puzzle. You really cannot say whose history is the more important. Imagine a four-dimensional puzzle of the world, and each of these different views of history is a piece of the puzzle. Before you can place them properly, though, you first must gather the pieces, and you do this by studying them all.

CONNECT YOUR KNOWLEDGE OF HISTORY
WITH YOUR TRAVEL.

I urge you, before you take your first overseas trip, to study the history of your destinations. Without the historical context, you will not be able to fully understand much of what you observe. You can be a tourist and enjoy the scenic sites, but understanding is a far richer experience. It doesn't matter where you start. Choose a country, then go there to see the truth for yourself.

HISTORY WILL SHOW YOU WHICH
FORCES DRIVE MARKETS.

By cross-referencing historical events with long-term trends in the market, you will identify those developments that affect stock and commodity prices. In my course "Bull and Bear" at Columbia University, I instructed students to research major bullish and bearish markets of the past, then figure out how they could have predicted the rises and falls in advance. What was going on in the world when prices skyrocketed or plummeted? Why did those events serve as a catalyst? Looking back upon history is an invaluable way to learn how to analyze trends. And better still, it teaches you how to anticipate future changes.

NOTHING IS REALLY NEW.

History repeats itself in one way or another—or at least rhymes, as Mark Twain said. Human beings have pretty much always been the same. Headlines are constantly announcing the innovative, the radical, and the groundbreaking. When something is presented as novel or different, look to the past, and you will always find a precedent there. But remember the historical context; don't expect things to be identical. A general rule: What is happening now has happened before and will happen again.

By way of illustration, take the Internet revolution. Many people reacted as though something entirely new had emerged. The Net is but one of many technological innovations to have presented themselves over history. Remember the "new economy" of the 1990s? Those with historical perspective can point to many such revolutions: the railroad, the clipper ship, airplanes, electricity, radio, telephone, television, the computer. Investments in all of those "new eras," at one time or another, ended badly.

As soon as I hear everyone making claims for something that supposedly is innovative and unprecedented, I check whether the market is overheated and often pull out my capital. Be extremely doubtful when you have people proclaiming, "It's different this time." Historically, nothing emerges as so entirely different; such claims are indicative of a state of mass hysteria. I sold short shares in high technology between 1999 and 2000, and it was right around that time that the commodity index I created in 1998 started to rise.

Again, study history very carefully. Learn precisely what happened and what did not. This will help you understand what is *about* to happen in the world.

CHAPTER 8

Your Education, Part IV: Learn Languages (and Make Sure That Mandarin Is One of Them!)

MANDARIN WILL BE THE NEXT GLOBAL LANGUAGE.

People who can speak or read other languages have a great advantage over those who don't. When it comes to investing, you can research primary sources and speak to people in their own language, increasing the likelihood of trust and candor. Just as important, there will be times in your life when you will be in social and professional situations with people from other cultures. Your life will be enriched immeasurably if you can defy the stereotype that Americans don't learn other languages and put yourself in a position to learn from your new friends.

To help you succeed in life as well as investing, we gave you a head start. You have a Chinese governess who communicates with you in the official language of China. And as you learn Mandarin from her, you will learn English from us. (You must master English to speak to your father; about the only expression he knows in Chinese is "cold beer.") We moved to Asia so that both of you could attend Chinese schools and use Mandarin in everyday life while experiencing both Asian and Western cultures.

Probably the best advice I can give to anyone, anywhere in the world, is to have your children and grandchildren learn Mandarin. For their generation, Mandarin and English will be the most important languages in the world.

CHAPTER 9

It Is the Century of China

PAY ATTENTION TO THE MAJOR CHANGES
TAKING PLACE IN THE WORLD NOW.

The reason that you are learning Mandarin is because China is gaining economic, political, and cultural strength, and will become an even more significant player internationally. You must be aware of such developments, not only as an investor but as a world citizen. When we look back upon history, we know that Spain dominated the sixteenth century, while France was the more prosperous country two hundred years later. The nineteenth century was the century of Great Britain. In the twentieth century, the United States rose to prominence. Well, the twenty-first century belongs to China.

This development is under way now, right before our eyes. China has had recurring periods of greatness. Egypt was great once, Rome was great once, Great Britain was great once. China has done it a few times and has weathered disasters a few times. Now it is on the rise again after three hundred years of decline.

The Chinese are generally considered Communists, not capitalists, but how accurate is this? Historically, the Chinese people have been among the best capitalists in the world. Many remember the form of capitalism that existed in China prior to Mao Tse-tung's revolution in 1949, which culminated in the founding of the People's Republic of China. Those who would not give up on capitalism during the revolution fled to Hong Kong, Taiwan, America, and elsewhere, and cultivated their own economic prosperity. These overseas ethnic Chinese have always been a valuable asset to China. They know the language and pass it down to later generations as well as retain ties to other Chinese on the mainland and around the world. They are always ready with capital and expertise to invest back in China as opportunities arise. The bond has always been so great that China gives passports to those of Chinese descent even if they have been away for a few generations.

There is a remarkable difference between the China that I saw in my first four visits between 1984 and 1990 and the China that I saw when I traveled there in 1999. The effort that the country has put into increasing its productivity has paid off. China's production levels in home electrical appliances, cellular phones, and motorcycles have surpassed those of the United States. In fact, China's cell phone production is now tops in the world. These are developments that an investor cannot dismiss.

BUY CHINESE STOCKS, AND BUY THE
FUTURE OF THIS COUNTRY!

I own two or three dozen Chinese stocks, but I did not make my first purchase until 1988. This happened in a run-down building, then the home of the Shanghai Stock Exchange. The bank-stock certificate representing that initial purchase hangs framed on a wall in our house. I don't know by how much its value has increased, but I have no intention of selling it because of its sentimental value.

When I revisited Shanghai in 1999, the shabby building had been replaced by a brand-new structure. I opened up an account and continued to invest more. China's gross national product (GNP) has grown in excess of 9 percent, and there is plenty of potential for further growth.

Many famous American investors who rarely, if ever, invested abroad or invested in China have done so in this decade because of the enormous growth. But if you want to buy Chinese stocks, be prepared for the normal setbacks in the Chinese economy. The United States underwent many consolidations as it rose to power and glory, and China will too. When is the best time to sell? Probably not until after my lifetime, because the Chinese economy will continue to grow. So my shares in China may be my gift to you.

A HARD LANDING CANNOT BE AVOIDED!

Both the Chinese economy and Chinese real estate became overheated, with an inflation rate somewhere between 7 percent and 8 percent, according to independent banks. Perhaps Chinese banks made too many loans. Excessive investment resulted in a higher than normal default rate, which usually happens in periods like this. I think that a hard landing in some sectors, such as real estate, is inevitable.

The Chinese government and the International Monetary Fund (IMF) insist that a soft landing is possible, and the Chinese government restricted bank loans for awhile and restrained the money supply, rightly to cool things off. Low interest rates have led to overinvestment in real estate and certain manufacturing industries. These sectors are taking a nosedive. Other fields, however, will probably be unaffected.

A Japanese investor once asked me when China was going to experience its hard landing. I explained that there is no telling exactly when that will be or how severe it will be. I am not a trader with a superior sense of timing. It could happen soon, or it may not happen at all. It is more likely to occur in specific sectors such as real estate, while some sectors will not be affected. But who knows? As soon as you hear in the news about a hard landing in the Chinese economy similar to those in 1989 and 1994, consider it the best opportunity to buy into Chinese stocks or commodities. I began buying Chinese shares again at the end of 2005 and into 2006, and again in late 2008 for the first time since 1999.

CHINA EQUALS COMMODITIES.

The rise of China brings with it a rise in demand for commodities. China, with its 1.3 billion people, consumes steel, iron ore, and soy; it is the largest consumer of copper in the world and the second leading consumer of energy, including oil. Furthermore, the demand is increasing yearly—monthly, even. It will take who knows how many years before supply meets demand; in the interim, this imbalance will continue to drive up the price of commodities despite the normal, periodic corrections to prices.

CHAPTER 10

Know Thyself by Understanding Your Weaknesses and Acknowledging Your Mistakes

KNOW WHO YOU ARE.

Of course you need to be aware of the circumstances that surround you, you need to be knowledgeable about the world, you need to know history. But even more important, you need to know yourself. Look at yourself in the mirror and ask what drives you. If you can understand these things up front, you are more likely to be able to keep your head in a crisis. Also observe how you react to mistakes, so that you can respond more constructively the next time things go wrong.

For example, I know now that I often see things well before others and therefore act much too soon. So I have tried to discipline myself to wait. When I was younger, I nearly always got swept away when stocks were rising amid mass hysteria or when people were dumping in panic. I often joined in too. I have learned that when I am frantic to join a trend, I must steel myself to do the opposite. It is extremely difficult to say "buy" when everyone else is selling and I am desperate to join in, but I have learned a bit about my own emotions over the years.

Granted, we all make mistakes. The important thing about making errors in judgment is the ability to admit those errors. If you grow into adulthood unable to acknowledge your mistakes—in life, as well as in investing—you will learn your lessons the hard way. Only when you recognize your mistakes will you be able to make the corrections necessary to put yourself on the right path.

PEOPLE ARE EASILY CARRIED AWAY
BY MOB PSYCHOLOGY.

Even those who call themselves professionals are at times persuaded by the mob. I remember when I started full-time on Wall Street in 1968, during another period of mania, I shared an office with an older analyst because things were growing so fast that companies could not even get more office space (a sign of trouble, I now know). I was diligently working out some numbers on a spreadsheet when an executive rushed into the office to see the analyst. When he saw what I was doing, he exclaimed, "Do people still waste time on things like that?!" I was mortified, of course, but that executive was out of the business just a few months later when that little bubble popped.

More recently, a number of "experts" lost a lot of money in the dot-com and credit debacles. You can imagine how hard it was for people who saw a bubble coming to pick up the paper every day and realize that people were getting rich (at least on paper) all around them. Maybe this really was a New Era, and the old rules did not apply. Whenever we enter a so-called new era, folks start to ignore decades-old standards of valuations for investments because they believe the growth will be so dazzling that stocks will trade at unbelievable prices and then will triple and quadruple again. Classic measures like book value, earnings per share, and dividends will be ignored and even ridiculed.

The *Wall Street Journal* began referring to the New Economy in the late 1990s because, it claimed, "things have changed so much." Companies with no history, low sales, and no earnings went public on the stock exchanges and shot up in price. Thousands of multimillionaires were created overnight. People projected huge growth in earnings for years into the future. In the end, of course, the old rules did apply, and many folks learned this the hard way. The *Wall Street Journal* went back to using lowercase letters the few times it mentioned the (ahem) new economy. Many companies collapsed and disappeared—just as always has happened after all the "new eras" in history.

For another example, look at Japan. In 2002 and 2003,

most analysts and economists discouraged investment in Japanese stocks, some going so far as to claim that investors should sell every Japanese stock they owned and some even suggested that Japanese leave Japan altogether. Such misguided advice was born of mob psychology; the gloom had become so deep-rooted that not even the professionals could see the changes taking place before them.

Japan had enjoyed a huge bubble in the 1980s. When it burst, in 1990, prices collapsed, sending the economy tumbling. Regrettably, the government and the Bank of Japan kept trying to halt the natural, cleansing effects of this recession by propping up many of the companies in trouble. Just as a forest fire serves to clear out deadwood and underbrush so that the forest can renew itself, recessions help to ensure healthy future growth. In Japan, businesses that should have been liquidated became "zombie companies," surviving, albeit barely, on the government's artificial support. Everything was Band-Aided with quick fixes. While this delayed a decline, it also postponed the economy's recovery. A country can actually spend more money trying to stave off a recession than the recession itself might cost. Moreover, most developed nations now have safety nets in place to limit the damage from a recession.

Japan still talks of the 1990s as "the lost decade," characterized by no washout, but no recovery, either. (By the way, America followed the same route in the 1970s, and endured a miserable decade until a new policy helped the country finally start over. One would think that central bankers would learn their lessons from history, but, unfortunately, the United States is again repeating the same mistakes, and America may be in for an extended period of difficult economic times.) Now, bear in mind that lifetime employment with the same company had been a longstanding foundation of Japanese society. When companies had to lay off workers in the nineties, an unprecedented development, the country practically fell into a national depression—reflected in low birth rates and a disturbingly high suicide rate.

It took thirteen years of stagnation, but finally, around 2003, the Japanese economy started to rebound. Then the stock market there doubled.

DO NOT PANIC; LEARN THE PSYCHOLOGY.

To be a successful investor, you really need to understand psychology as well as history and philosophy. Very often emotions drive the market up or down. Remember that *economies* and *stock markets* are two different things. As Paul Samuelson, the Nobel Prize–winning economist, once put it, "The stock market has anticipated nine of the last five recessions." China's economy, for example, has been growing rapidly for years now, yet its stock market declined consistently for *four years* between 2001 and 2005. The public, overreacting to positive or negative news reports, will buy or sell short at the wrong time. Investor psychology can accelerate such trends in the market.

Anybody can feel panicky. I have panicked a number of times and lost money in the market. After the oil shock of 1978 to 1980, when oil prices doubled, I watched the price of oil continue to rise. My research told me that, with supply exceeding demand, the price would soon fall, and so I ended up selling short. Just then, war broke out between Iran and Iraq, two of the world's largest oil producers. With the world concerned about possible future oil shortages, prices only shot up further.

I had to admit the error in judgment. Some called it bad luck, but no. I didn't do my homework. I should have seen the conflict between these two foes coming. *Someone* had to know that war was imminent. Huge military movements had to have occurred. Propaganda machines had to have been activated. Much like a novice trader, I then had to scramble to buy back the position I had sold, and at a higher price than before. The oil price eventually fell, as I predicted it would, but by then, it was too late: I had already closed out my position.

In hindsight, I should not have panicked. I should have realized that the fundamentals underpinning the oil price weren't sound. I had not quite grasped the effect of the mob mentality at the time, and as a result, I made a costly mistake. Losing your perspective in the midst of market panic is equivalent to losing your money in that market.

SELLING HYSTERIA.

For the most part, it is in short-term trades that prices are driven by emotion. Mid-term and long-term investments are usually influenced more by the fundamentals. Ordinarily I do not use charts to trade. Now, some people in the markets use graphs of previous stock or commodity movements in order to predict future price movements. They are called "technicians" or "chartists." They spend a lot of time poring over the historic price movements and the formations these show on their charts as a way to predict what will happen next. Occasionally, I will turn to them as a way to see what has been happening and to check facts if I sense mob hysteria or panic at work. Charts sometimes reveal a beeline rise, an indication that prices have increased far beyond actual value. It means that people have lost perspective. It shows the level of the hysteria. I know that prices will eventually return to the appropriate level, so I sell short. You need to be careful, though, that you are not selling short simply because prices are high. Never sell short unless prices are astronomically expensive, *and* you detect negative change coming.

Recently, pending evidence of hysteria in the charts for certain stocks related to home building, I sold them short. What I want you to remember is that bubbles burst in the wake of hysteria, while plummeting prices usually end in panic. You can see panic in falling prices when you see them collapsing straight down day after day for extended periods. Historically, long periods of selling have ended in "selling climaxes" when everyone finally panics and dumps to get out of the market at any price no matter what the fundamental reality might be. Large price declines across the board should attract your attention. A good rule of thumb is to sell during times of market hysteria and buy during times of panic. Always remember to *buy low* and *sell high*. It sounds so simple, but it is extremely difficult. Just keep this dictum in mind always—especially when your emotions are getting the best of you.

CHAPTER 11

Recognize Change and Embrace It

EVERYTHING CHANGES.
EVERYTHING.

To understand what is likely to happen in the future, you have to be able to understand current events and the changes presently under way in the world. All social environments transform over time. Some people see such changes as evidence of a society's opening up, others as a reflection of its closing in. Regardless of your perspective, refusing to accept the change is like swimming against the current of a thundering river. Try to resist the force, and you will not last very long.

NO ONE HAS DEFIED THE PRINCIPLE OF
SUPPLY AND DEMAND AND SURVIVED.

In 1991 the world witnessed a significant change: the fall of the Soviet Union. The totalitarian state was unable to sustain its political framework because of the fatal flaw of Communism, an ideology purposely deaf to the fundamental principle that you can find on the first page of any economics textbook: supply and demand.

It is only logical that Communism would fail. All prices fluctuate according to supply and demand. Therefore sustaining a distorted pricing structure for any length of time is impossible, even if restricted to just one country. No government, no empire, has ever defied the principle of supply and demand and prevailed. In 1990, I traveled by motorcycle through the cities of the Soviet Union. Gloom (and not just the perennially gray Russian skies) permeated everywhere I went. I felt as though I was actually seeing Communism on the brink of collapse. Two years later, the USSR dissolved.

CHANGE CAN BE A CATALYST.

When I give advice about investing, I always emphasize the need to recognize change. Successful investors manage to do this—in most cases buying stock, commodities, currencies, bonds, real estate, art, antiques, coins, stamps, collectibles, and so on at phenomenally cheap prices, putting very little money at risk.

But a cheap price alone is not sufficient reason to invest. If something is forever cheap, then it has no recognized value, and its stock may very well remain a worthless piece of paper. For a bargain to soar in price, there has to be a catalyst, and from an investment perspective, that catalyst is change. Whatever the change may be, it must have a significant impact within a country or an industry, and it must also be recognized as significant externally within a few years. If the change is real, others will notice the improvement, and prices will rise to reflect the new circumstances. New investors will catch on and prices can rise considerably for years.

DEALING WITH CHANGE.

So how do you deal with change? I am referring not to superficial changes, but to fundamental transformations that happen maybe once in the course of decades.

When I was a child, immediately after World War II, America was the richest, most powerful country in the world. Now we are the largest debtor nation in history and are terribly overextended in many ways. When my grandfather returned home in 1918 after having served as a fighter pilot in World War I, the United Kingdom was still widely regarded as the richest, most powerful nation on earth, yet few saw the changes taking place beneath the surface.

Within just one generation, it lost its empire and became a financial mess.

Will you adapt to the changes happening around you, or will you resist the changes and lament the passing of "better days" long gone? I hope the former! Those who cannot adjust to change will be swept aside by it. Those who recognize change and react accordingly will benefit.

CHAPTER 12

Look to the Future!

EVERYONE WOULD BE A MILLIONAIRE IF HE COULD
READ A NEWSPAPER FROM THE FUTURE.

When I was in my late twenties, working at Neuberger &
Berman, a supervisor said to me while reading his morning
paper, "When the market opens, Jim, there should be one
hundred thousand shares of X Company to be sold at price
Y, so I want you to buy those stocks." True enough, when
the market opened, there was a sell order for that exact
number of shares and at almost the exact price that he had
stipulated. He was able to figure out what was about to happen just by reading the newspaper and sensing the mood of
the market. To this day, I remain impressed.

People who can observe events as they unfold will certainly acquire wealth. After touring the world from 1990 to 1992, I wrote my first book, *Investment Biker*. Recently a reporter remarked to me how many of the predictions I made in that book had come true, such as the rise of nationalism and militant Islam. How was I able to foresee the future? he wanted to know. I simply did what an experienced investor did: I read the news.

My motorcycle journey coincided with the end of the Cold War, the struggle between Communism and capitalism. As I traveled through the Communist bloc, I could see that the national boundaries the USSR had forced upon divergent ethnic groups were unraveling. It seemed logical that without the political and ideological framework of Soviet Communism, these different groups would eventually insist on their own identity, founded upon ethnicity or religion or language. I reached this conclusion by way of my longstanding interest in history and philosophy. Only in this case, instead of reading the newspaper, I relied on my firsthand observation of the developments in these regions as they actually happened.

MANY COUNTRIES WILL COME APART.

A hundred years from now, there will probably be anywhere between three hundred and four hundred sovereign nations on this earth, almost twice as many as there are now.

Today people the world over drive Toyotas, dance to the

music of the pop star du jour, and dine on McDonald's and Chinese food, but such changes have had a wearying effect on certain groups of people. Such people are seeking alternatives, looking to have more control over their lives. No longer restricted by the ideological framework forced upon them by a totalitarian government, many are looking to religious, tribal, ethnic, and linguistic affiliations through which to express their identities. This will eventually result in subsequent redrawings of national borders, and a more fragmented, complex world. The empires and large nation-states that have built up over the past few decades often do not work and will come undone. This could be done peacefully, however, and does not necessarily insure war. For example, in 1993 Czechoslovakia split into the Czech Republic and Slovakia without bloodshed. Let us hope for the best going forward, since smaller, more responsive governments would be better for us all. Unfortunately, history shows that politicians usually bungle things.

Predictions: Iraq will ultimately divide according to religious sects into three or four countries. Canada, Russia, India, Brazil, and the Democratic Republic of the Congo may also split up. An understanding of history and an astute reading of the current course of events suggest that such developments are inevitable—and natural. Not one country in existence today has had the same borders and government for as long as two hundred years. The world will continue changing.

DO NOT PLACE YOUR BET ON THAT WHICH IS DYING OUT.

Keep your eye on the future. Do not cling to anything that will eventually cease to exist. No matter how much time or energy or money you invest in it, once something is gone, it is gone forever.

Several hundred years from now, there may be only thirty languages spoken in the world. Many languages will fall out of effective use in your lifetime. Those likely to be spoken for another several hundred years include English, Chinese, and Spanish. If you really want to succeed in the world, gamble on what you know will survive.

THE WOMEN'S ERA IS APPROACHING!

Traditionally, women in Asia have been treated differently from men. In many countries, a girl's family had to pay a dowry when she married as a further inducement to find her a husband. Like women everywhere, Asian women have long suffered a lack of equal opportunity in society; they have been treated unfairly in pay and promotion in the workplace. But this is all going to change. In China, Korea, India, and other Asian countries, where the priority has been placed on the birth of boys, girls are now in short supply. Soon the typical Asian man will experience great difficulty in finding a wife. For instance, in South Korea, there are 120 twenty-year-old boys for every 100 twenty-year-old girls, while in China, the birthrate is 119 boys for every 100 girls. As all these girls become women, they'll be able to demand more freedom. The ramifications from this will be enormous: Professions, education, politics, everything will change. I am so pleased to have two daughters!

PAY ATTENTION TO WHAT
EVERYBODY ELSE NEGLECTS.

Most investors look only to strong markets. By 1998 my research indicated that a commodities era was approaching. At the time, very few people noticed that the long downturn in the commodities market had severely limited supply. A reporter asked me what I thought was the best option for private investors. I pushed the sugar on the table toward her, smiled, and said, "*This* is the best investment. Take it home." The price of sugar at the time was 5.5 cents per pound. The reporter had looked at me skeptically; I smiled back at her. Sometimes, the more ridiculous an investment sounds to other people, the better the chances that it will yield a profit.

If you are looking for success, be quick to start something new, something that no one else has tried. And if you want to invest, look for the bear market. Many have frequently profited by investing where no one else saw potential—

putting money into commodities in 1998, for example. You can be rich if you have the courage to buy something while it is still under the radar of conventional wisdom.

Incidentally, the price of sugar eventually tripled. But I'll bet that nice reporter missed her opportunity to make some serious money.

THE MORE CERTAIN SOMETHING IS, THE LESS LIKELY IT IS TO BE PROFITABLE.

A lot of people who attend my lectures ask me if one investment or another will "definitely" be profitable, or when exactly they should buy and sell. Whenever anyone asks me whether something is a sure bet, I tell them honestly that I simply do not know. Nothing in this world is absolutely certain, except my love for you, my daughters. When many people are absolutely sure of something, you should be suspicious.

DO NOT THINK IN TERMS OF WHAT YOU WISH.

Never act upon wishful thinking. Act without checking the facts, and chances are that you will be swept away along with the mob. Whenever you see people acting in the same way, it is time to investigate supply and demand objectively.

Let me give you an example: In 1980 everybody wanted to own gold. The price had skyrocketed to over $850 per troy ounce. But one could see that gold was being overproduced; after all, a supplier is bound to increase production for anything that rises in price. A lot of people bought gold at this inflated price, insisting that it was somehow different from other commodities. Boy, were they wrong.

More gold started to be mined, and, at the same time, the demand for the precious metal scaled back. In fact, many folks who owned gold jewelry sold it to refiners for melting, which further increased the supply. By the year 2000, the price of gold had sunk to about $250 an ounce. History shows that most bubbles take years for recovery, so there is rarely any reason to rush in after a period of mania. The exact same change in supply and demand happened with silver, which tumbled from $50 in 1980 during its mania to under $4 a couple of decades later.

When you see so many people being unrealistic, stop and make an objective assessment of the supply-and-demand equation. Bearing in mind this basic principle will bring you that much closer to success.

KNOW WHEN NOT TO DO ANYTHING.

Anytime that you think you've become a financial genius— when, in fact, you simply have had the good luck to turn a profit—it is time to sit back and do nothing for a while. If you stumble upon success in a bull market and decide that you are gifted, stop right there. Investing at that point is dangerous, because you are starting to think like everybody else. Wait until the mob psychology that is influencing you subsides.

CHAPTER 13

Lady Luck Smiles on Those Who Continue in Their Efforts

DO YOUR HOMEWORK, OR YOU WILL
END UP WITH A GLASS BEAD.

Once you take that first step toward your dream, put your full effort into it. Do your homework. If you want to succeed, you must never neglect it. My most successful investments were those in which I invested the most time and hard work, collecting all available information and researching every detail. If you don't understand something—I mean truly understand it—you will never be successful. Likewise, if you merely dabble in an area, you are gambling, not investing.

When your mother and I were circumnavigating the

globe, I bought her a diamond from some smugglers in Namibia, Africa. They told me that the diamond was worth $70,000. I bargained the price down to a mere $500 because I thought the sellers were desperate. Immediately upon seeing it, your mother pronounced that I had been taken. Later, in Tanzania, I showed my purchase to a diamond trader. He laughed, because it was not a diamond but a glass bead. Of course, I knew the value of diamonds, but their value is all I knew. I was such an amateur that I could not tell the difference between a real diamond and a fake! All this time I had been advising people to invest only in what they know, and here I'd made a complete fool of myself over diamonds.

You have to know what you are dealing with if you want to be successful. If you do not know how to tell if a diamond is genuine, you are going to end up as I did: with a glass bead. Looking back on it, I am glad that it was not the real thing. It was a relatively inexpensive reminder for me to avoid investing in anything that I do not completely understand!

THE ARROGANT ARE BLIND TO THE TRUTH.

If you let vanity and self-importance take over, you will lose all that you have achieved. And fast.

You need only look at the United States. Some Americans have no interest in the world yet believe they are the center of it. They just do not understand why the United States has ceased to be as competitive as it once was. They believe that devaluing the currency is the key to selling American products. With that kind of logic, there is no way that the U.S. dollar can remain strong for very long.

Throughout history, many countries have tried debasing their currency as a way to revive the economy by making it a bit more competitive. It has never worked over the long run or even intermediately. It *can* work in the short term, but not always. Only quality and service work over time.

Ignorance is born of an outsized sense of self-importance. Never let yourself become arrogant. Study hard. The more you learn, the more you will realize how little you know—and armed with this humility, you will never lose sight of the distance that separates self-confidence and self-importance.

DO NOT STOP WHEN YOU ARE WORKING TOWARD YOUR DREAM.

While I was driving around the world with your mother, my father's cancer deteriorated and he eventually passed away. But I did not stop our journey to return to my father's side. That might sound selfish or coldhearted. And so I want you to know why I made this choice. For me to go on a round-the-world trip was my father's dream as well as mine. *He* insisted that I not cut the trip short for his sake. When his condition worsened, it was important to me to tell him how proud of him I was and how much I loved him. I phoned Dad frequently and wrote him numerous letters. But I did not return to the United States. I still cry about it when I remember those days and his wishes.

I want you to fulfill your dreams. That is my dream too. As your father, I wish for you a lifetime of happiness and fulfillment. I want you to pursue, without pause, whatever it is that stirs your passion. Keep working toward your dream, not someone else's, and not mine, either. A lot of people try to live for others—their children, their spouses, their parents, their friends—and in doing so twist themselves into knots attempting to meet their often outsized and/or unrealistic expectations. That leaves little space for personal growth and progress, and creates resentment for lost opportunities.

I will always offer you advice about what I think you should do, but the decision is yours about whether or not to accept it! I do not want you to live your lives for me. Because I love you, I encourage you to be true to yourselves. Every effort that you make to live to the fullest only deepens my affection for you. I am your father, but you need to set your own goals, envision your own futures, and find your own paths. I will do my best to help you avoid mistakes, but I know that you will make some anyway. I would do anything to prevent you from suffering setbacks or hurts; that's what fathers do. (I mean, I still cringe every time one of you winces during a vaccination.) What I'm trying to say is that in the end, your success and happiness are up to you!

You both probably will marry some day. I made a couple of mistakes in this area so I know how debilitating this can be. I had acted despite my own doubts and judgment, so I acted foolishly, at least partly because I felt it was too late to back out. Your mother was smarter in what is often the single most important decision in a person's life. Be extremely careful—even reluctant—before marrying. Do not do it if you have any doubts at all even if it means walking away from the altar at the last minute. Your mother and I will always stand by you.

PASS THIS MESSAGE ON TO *YOUR* CHILD.

I really look forward to conveying to you lessons that my parents and grandparents taught me. I know that raising both of you will be the ultimate adventure of my life. Happy, when you were still in your mother's womb, I bought a map of the world and a globe for you, along with a piggy bank. Of course, I have done the same for Baby Bee. I hope that someday you'll share with your own children the wisdom that your mother and I have imparted to you.

Epilogue

The devil of life is always in the details, so I thought I'd close by giving you a series of little rules that have guided me well.

Always buy quality products. They last longer and retain more value.

Always eat before you go grocery shopping! If you're hungry when you go, you'll end up buying more food than you need!

Anything that is a "must see," "must try," "must read," should almost certainly be avoided, especially if it is popular.

Use good manners no matter where you are or whom you meet. They are an eternal verity that will always distinguish you. Be sensitive to the mores of each society because "good manners" are often different in various cultures.

Beware of all politicians everywhere. They excelled at recess when they were in school but have excelled at little since.

Never ask someone how much money he or she makes, or how much something costs. Never tell someone how much *your* things cost. Never discuss how much money you make or have. My parents and grandparents ingrained this in me because it is ostentatious and poor manners, at least for us. Prove yourself by your actions rather than by talking about money. There are many folks these days who love discussing their money and flashing it about, but it is not the way I hope you will live.

If and when you borrow money, pay it back on time, if not in advance. Good credit is vital. A bad credit record will haunt you for years.

As you get older, you will have to deal with boys. I expect always to be giving you advice and warning you about boys. The basic principle to remember is this: They need you more than you need them. They will make you millions of promises in their frantic pursuit of you. Take it from someone who knows; I can tell the stories better than they can. Just ignore them and stay true to yourself. Use your common sense when you start hearing absurd promises, compliments, and flattery. Do not follow a boy to a different school, city, or job. Make the boys follow *you*.

When you get older, remember that you will gain little from singles bars—the bartenders will learn and earn more from the experience than you will.

Be wary: Learn that many men who look old enough to be your father or grandfather do not think of you as their daughter or granddaughter.

Do not get married until you are at least twenty-eight and know a bit more about yourself and the world.

It is vitally important to maintain boundaries between work and life. Skip going out for drinks with the gang after work every night. You will notice that the boss does not do it, which is one reason that he is the boss. And while we are discussing the boss: There is rarely, if ever, any sound reason for you to have a drink with him or her alone, much less dinner. And while we are discussing drinking, never drink at a business lunch. Finally, and importantly, avoid in-office romances. They usually end in personal and professional disaster for one or both parties.

Always use the toilet before you set out on a long drive or make an appearance in public.

Learn to type and to sew. I never did, and I regret it often, on both counts.

Learn to do as much arithmetic and figures as possible in your head. This may sound strange, considering that calculators are everywhere, but you will have a leg up by understanding the numbers better than others, while also noticing anomalies others miss. Besides, what will they do when they've left their calculators at home? This will be a huge advantage for you as few will be able to keep up with you.

Finally, take care of yourself! It's difficult to be successful if you aren't healthy and rested. You know how your mother is always putting sunscreen on you? She is exactly right.

Learn to stay calm—especially in times of pressure or turmoil. You will make much better decisions plus everyone will soon notice you are calm under pressure when others are not. I have gotten better, but still am a hothead too often—and always regret it later.

Always be early for appointments. You will be much more efficient with your time and will make a very good impression since many arrive late—some repeatedly late.

Once you do get to know and understand yourself, *remember* who you are and stay with it. I still get carried away at times and act emotionally or do things at which I am not good. I always look back and try to kick myself into remembering I need to be true to myself. For example, I some-times jump into an investment when it is moving up only to remember later it was emotion overcoming my own self awareness. I *always* regret it when I do not stay with my own best abilities—whether in investing or anything else.

I have learned in life that being greedy nearly always causes problems. An old Wall Street adage says: Bulls make money; bears make money. Pigs go broke.

Always ask questions and never be afraid to do so. The only dumb question is the one you do not ask.

For more wisdom and advice from Jim Rogers,
visit www.jimrogers.com.

Born on October 19, 1942, JIM ROGERS had his first job at age five, picking up bottles at baseball games. After growing up in Demopolis, Alabama, he won a scholarship to Yale University. Upon graduation, he attended Balliol College at the University of Oxford, where he earned his first Guinness record as coxswain of the rowing crew. He cofounded the Quantum Fund, a global investment partnership. During the 1970s, the portfolio grew 4,200 percent, while the S&P rose less than 47 percent. Rogers then decided to retire—at age thirty-seven—but he did not remain idle.

Continuing to manage his own portfolio, Rogers served as a professor of finance at the Columbia University Graduate School of Business and as a moderator of *The Dreyfus Roundtable* on WCBS-TV and *The Profit Motive* on FNN. At the same time, he laid the groundwork for his lifelong dream: an around-the-world motorcycle trip of more than one hundred thousand miles across six continents, his second Guinness record. That journey became the subject of Rogers's first book, *Investment Biker* (1994).

Rogers's Millennium Adventure 1999–2002, his third Guinness record, took him and his wife, Paige, through 116 countries (and about fifteen civil wars) and over 152,000 miles. His second book, *Adventure Capitalist,* chronicled that incredible journey.

He lives in Singapore with his wife and daughters and is a worldwide investor, media commentator, and lecturer.

He can be reached at www.jimrogers.com.

ABOUT THE TYPE

This book was set in Sabon, a typeface designed by
the well-known German typographer Jan Tschichold
(1902–1974). Sabon's design is based upon the original letterforms of Claude Garamond and was created
specifically to be used for three sources: foundry
type for hand composition, Linotype, and Mono-
type. Tschichold named his typeface for the famous
Frankfurt typefounder Jacques Sabon, who died in
1580.